T0129571

30 DAYS OF POSITIVE THINKING

A "How-to-Feel-Happy" Guide

GUNHILD "GIGI" DESILETS

BALBOA.
PRESS

A DIVISION OF HAY HOUSE

Copyright © 2019 Gunhild "Gigi" Desilets.

All rights reserved. No part of this book may be used or reproduced by
any means, graphic, electronic, or mechanical, including photocopying,
recording, taping or by any information storage retrieval system
without the written permission of the author except in the case
of brief quotations embodied in critical articles and reviews.

Balboa Press books may be ordered through booksellers or by contacting:

Balboa Press
A Division of Hay House
1663 Liberty Drive
Bloomington, IN 47403
www.balboapress.com
1 (877) 407-4847

Because of the dynamic nature of the Internet, any web addresses or
links contained in this book may have changed since publication and
may no longer be valid. The views expressed in this work are solely those
of the author and do not necessarily reflect the views of the publisher,
and the publisher hereby disclaims any responsibility for them.

The author of this book does not dispense medical advice or prescribe the use
of any technique as a form of treatment for physical, emotional, or medical
problems without the advice of a physician, either directly or indirectly. The
intent of the author is only to offer information of a general nature to help
you in your quest for emotional and spiritual well-being. In the event you use
any of the information in this book for yourself, which is your constitutional
right, the author and the publisher assume no responsibility for your actions.

Any people depicted in stock imagery provided by Getty Images are
models, and such images are being used for illustrative purposes only.
Certain stock imagery © Getty Images.

Print information available on the last page.

ISBN: 978-1-9822-2422-6 (sc)
ISBN: 978-1-9822-2423-3 (e)

Balboa Press rev. date: 03/25/2019

This book is for everyone with a dream of a better life - a life filled with joy, laughter, happiness, good health, abundance and fun times.

CONTENTS

INTRODUCTION

You attracted this book. You have asked for this positive thinking guide and now you are holding it in your hands (so celebrate!). This is the main message of this guide; what you think you will see as experiences in your life. Let me introduce myself. My name is Gunhild. I used to be a person stuck in negativity. I suffered from depression, anxiety, anorexia, negative thinking and suicide thoughts, and addictions to sex, cigarettes, drugs and alcohol. I have even been addicted to drama and chaos. I was stuck in a whirl wind of negative thoughts and feelings and I did not know how to get out of it. Then one day I woke up feeling sick and tired of being sick and tired. I knew I wanted change. I had no idea the amazing things that were about to happen for me. Change became something I couldn't avoid anymore and I quickly found myself on a new path. The day I decided in my heart I needed change the Universe listened and delivered. Suddenly I found myself meeting the most amazing people offering me their time and wisdom. How did I deserve these gifts from these wonderful people? My inner calling called for them and they came as I am deserving of all that I dream. As I found myself surrounded by people that had what I wanted (happiness, joy, inner calm, good health, a good life) I closed my mouth and opened my ears. I used to talk way too much and I didn't listen enough. How can I possibly learn something about life if I am too busy talking to myself and others about how tough and hard life is? I learnt to listen....really LISTEN.

I learnt to let go more and more of ego (oh boy, how that hurts!) and I had to be willing to learn. I had to want to want to change. One of my mentors said; "If you want to change, you have to start with your thoughts first!" She continued; "Are you willing to change everything?" I broke down in tears and pushed out a broken YES. You see, I couldn't just change one thing and keep the rest of the drama. If I wanted change I had to change EVERYTHING. My mentor honestly shared she would spend her time on me IF I did exactly as she said. If not she wouldn't waste a second on me – she had more important things to do. She was honest and straight to the point. No learning moment should ever go to waste. I needed her and so she was put into my life. I judged her in my mind before someone suggested she could be of great help to me. I told myself there is nothing a person like that can teach me (you see, I used to be the Master of the Universe. I KNEW everything......I truly believed that. What an illusion I was living!). I couldn't be more wrong! This lady helped lift me out of the dark and she gave me tools that I use to this day when I find old negative thinking habits sneak in.

More and more people of importance were put on my path. I am still amazed when I meet people that are so full of love, compassion, inner peace, passion, honesty and wisdom. The world is apparently filled with human beings like this and I just had to open myself up to seeing them.

This handbook was put into my heart and mind as a dream shortly after I decided to let go of drugs and alcohol and to change my life (sobriety date February 26th 2006). I had been given a gift from my life teachers; how to feel joy and happiness on the inside no matter what is happening on the outside. It would be selfish of me to keep these tools only to myself. I knew I would write the handbook one sweet day when the time was right for me and you. First I had to meet some more mentors and teachers on my path of life. Then I had to be around my teachers with my ears open to receive their teachings. And then I had to put those teachings into practice in every situation in my life before I could go out and share with the world. And that time is NOW.

I was once told I will find all the secrets of the world in libraries. All my life teachers shared with me the importance of books. And the books they asked me to read are books on self-help, positive thinking, self-love, yoga, meditation, health and spirituality. My teachers invited me to read every day – preferably one chapter a day. And if I told myself I couldn't find time to a chapter a day I had no excuses to why I couldn't read a page, a paragraph or one sentence a day. So I jumped into book after book after book. And the books took me out of my head and into my body. I started living more in the now instead of in the past or future. One day I was handed a handbook with a religious focus. I found myself having a healthy addiction to this handbook as it came with positive and loving messages for each day of the month. The handbook quickly became a frequent traveler of my purse and I had it with me everywhere. I read it first thing in the morning and as often as I needed throughout my day in order to keep my positive focus. I realized this little handbook became a friend and loving support as I went through the roller coaster of change. I wanted the world to experience the same handbook the way I did, but I knew that not everyone would be open to the religious texts. So I decided I needed to create a handbook for everyone else that wanted to change negative thinking to positive thinking. Just because someone didn't believe in a religion I didn't think it was fair they would miss out on making friends with a handbook that could change their life.

The teachings in the book you now are holding are the result of me asking my Source to guide my words as I typed on my computer. As if someone led my fingers on the key board the words just started showing themselves on my laptop screen. I noticed Source came as "WE", so I have a feeling it is a gathering of energies that have come together and shown themselves as my inner truth. I asked my inner self to take the lead and put into writing the messages you needed. I need these messages as well – if not they wouldn't have been written. Because in my experience; the words I share as I teach my yoga classes or mentor someone are the ones I also need to hear. And it has been confirmed in my life that we are NEVER alone in what we are going through and there is always someone else who needs the same teaching as I do.

Another important reason why I want to share these techniques with you is because I missed learning about life in public schools. As a child and youth in school I found that no one taught about thoughts or emotions. The focus in school was on the outside of the body. Nothing was taught about those ten thousand thoughts I found myself experiencing daily. And no one taught me tools for dealing with negative thinking. The more and more I found myself questioning what adults stressed as important in life I grew more and more confused with the world. I had to become an adult before I found my life teachers. There are no words that can describe what they have done for me. They saved my life!

I am glad you are here. I am glad you are reading these words. You have already taken the first step toward change; you asked for change. And this guide is just one of many tools available for you on your path of letting go of negative thinking. Use this guide as a daily tool to keep you focused on something positive. Each day you wake let the motivation for that day (date) be the first thing your eyes read. And throughout your day refer back to the same page to keep that positivity fill your entire day. If you feel you need more messages that day simply hold the guide in your hands and ask the Universe to give you the right message by letting the pages glide between your fingers. Then open the book when it feels right and you have the message your soul needs. This is what you can do on the 31st of the month as well or simply read DAY 30 again. You see, there is something powerful in hearing the same message over and over again. Because each day you wake you are a new person. So each time you read a message you have read before you will find something new in that same message…..because you are new.

Please know you are very important to me and I am so grateful you are holding this book. Because in holding this book you are ready for practicing the tools and techniques in this guide. And when you do you become an even brighter light in the world for others to see. And for that I am forever grateful!

With much love and gratitude and light,
Gunhild "Gigi" Desilets

DAY 1

So you are ready for change? Good. It is in due time. You are here on this planet Earth to be the best version of you. This should be your goal. To be a better version of you today than you were yesterday. This takes work. Or as we prefer to call it; practice. Don't judge yourself when you fall. Because you will fall a lot in the beginning of creating change for yourself. We love that you fall. Rise one more time than you fell down and you will always find yourself standing tall. When you share with the Universe through your thoughts that you would like change…..get ready… because here it comes! It will feel like a tornado at first. Or even like a crazy roller coaster that never ends. This happens to everyone starting change. The ups and downs will slowly but surely start to even out. And you will be able to keep your calm no matter what the circumstances. This takes time. It takes practice. One step at a time. Suddenly as you ask change into your life, books, people, teachers and/or self-development opportunities will start to be shown to you. It is up to you which ones to follow. Listen to your gut feeling. The feeling in your stomach is your truth. Not all leads will be right for you, but they are there for you if you need them. Change is the only thing guaranteed in life. Birth is change. Death is change. Therefor life is change. Nothing stays the same. So just wait; and you will change too. It might be a tough road, but we know the path of change is worth it. Therefor we encourage you to find others going through change so you can relate to each other and support each other. We encourage you to find a mentor – someone who was been where you are now and was able to walk the path of change and is now living happily. And at one point in life, you will be that mentor to someone else. Because if you learn how to be happy and how to move through difficulty, it will be very selfish of you to keep that wisdom just to yourself. So one day, you will go on and share the wisdom that change gave you. Until then; open your ears and practice listening. And we say that we much love and respect. Because if you simply listen….truly listen….you might learn something. And in learning you grow. Learning is a part of walking the path of change. We wish you good luck and all the best! Because you deserve it!

Today's mantra: I OPEN MY HEART FOR CHANGE!

DAY 2

We are here to tell you that you are enough! Nothing is missing with you! You ARE! You simply are! What are things about you that you like? Focus on that! Why do you criticize yourself all the time? Yes! You do criticize yourself all the time! Stop it! It serves no purpose. Did we ask you to come here to be negative beings? NO! We asked you to come here to be positive beings. Fulfilled. Enough. You are enough! Who in your life right now tells you that you are not enough? You! No one else. Be your own best friend and you will always be happy. Yes! We said it; you will ALWAYS be happy if you become your own best friend. Life is about happiness! Not about lying to yourself about who you think you should be in the world. Simply BE! We are encouraging you to knock down all self-doubt with the strongest and most powerful tool in the entire UNIVERSE – your thoughts!

Today's mantra: I AM ENOUGH!

DAY 3

Where did you come from? Have you asked yourself that question lately? Why are you here? You are here in order to love. To love and to be loved. Be loved by you. Why you? Because if you don't love you, who will? Nobody. You might think you are in a healthy relationship and that you are with the love of your life when the relationship is new. But what happens after a while when those roses stop coming or those daily texts with "HOW ARE YOU TODAY, LOVE?" become less frequent? Too often you reach outside yourself to get validation that you are good enough, don't you? If someone tells you that you are wonderful and great and beautiful then it must be so. But what happens when those complements are non-existing or few and far in between? It is no one's job to love you or to give you compliments. It is your job! So start by saying nice things to yourself. Say it in your mind. No one can hear you but you. Your cells hear you. Your organs and your muscles and your bones hear you. Sweet talk yourself. Be nice to yourself. So what is today's mantra? You guessed it; I LOVE MYSELF!

DAY 4

So what is new? You are new. You are new each morning you rise. You are new with each breath. So why do you judge yourself based on what you said and did twenty years ago? Are others judging you based on what you did years or decades ago? Probably not. But if they are *they* are the ones being stuck in the past. Get out of your own past and start living in the NOW. So you said something ten years ago that hurt someone else and it hurt you. Ok, move on. If you apologized you can move on without guilt. If you didn't apologize, you still can. BUT only if saying sorry won't hurt anyone. Do you go ring the door of your old lover to say sorry in front of his or her children and family? NO! If it causes harm to say sorry now, you DON'T apologize in person. And you don't send a text or an email or a letter either. You simply live the situation in your mind; see yourself face to face to the person and say sorry in your mind. Then set an intention to never act in that way again and forgive yourself. Done deal! Move on! That is it! No more drama. LET IT GO! Simply let it go. It is when you hold on to bitterness towards yourself and others that YOU are stuck in your own past. Why would you do that to yourself? You are hurting yourself every single time you think of that situation! You re-live that situation sometimes daily! Stop it! Let go and let God! (You can exchange the word God for LOVE, SOURCE, TRUTH, ENERGY,

HIGHER POWER or any other word that pleases you.)
Move on! Be happy!

So today's mantra is a powerful one: I FORGIVE MYSELF!

GUNHILD "GIGI" DESILETS

DAY 5

What did you tell your body today? Did you talk nice to it? Or did you feed your body negative self-talk? You probably have judged your body several times today already. You judge yourself all the time — every day. You judge yourself when you look into the mirror, when you get a glimpse of yourself in the department store window and you judge yourself every time you take your clothes off. You criticize your toes, your fingernails, your hair, your back, your butt, your belly, and your knees. And we could go on and on listing every part of your body. Please stop criticizing yourself because you are making yourself ill. You know, your cells hear everything you say to yourself in your thoughts. Do you think that toe will change it's shape as long as you tell it how ugly it is every day? NO! You can change the way you feel about your body by changing how you speak to yourself about your own body. And perhaps the shape of your body will change as you change your words about your physical self. Or maybe it won't. Either way, the way you FEEL about yourself is key here. Your job is to walk around shining your light from the inside out. Your light won't be shining if you self-criticize and self-sabotage yourself through your thoughts. What is on the inside will shine out. ALWAYS! Your job is to observe your thoughts and your words. Be nice to yourself and others will start to be nice to you. Let's start simple. Let's start with this simple mantra:

I LOVE YOU, BODY! I TRUST YOU, BODY! THANK YOU, BODY!

DAY 6

We love you! We want you to know that. Do you love yourself? Every day you wake up we want for you to wake up happy about who you are. In order for that to be easy for you (because you have to admit you don't always find that easy; loving yourself) a few things have to happen inside your thoughts. You need to find acceptance of who you are. You need to find acceptance of who you have been. Don't be mad or bitter about your own doing in the past. It is in the past; not here and now. UNLESS you re-live it in your mind over and over again. Then it is here all over again! Stop doing that! Find time in your days to come to sit in silence and simply breathe. Simply listen to the sound of your breath. If you are not familiar with yoga breath, we highly suggest you go online and find a how-to-instructions to do yoga breath. This breath is essential and very beneficial for your health – body, mind and soul. So sit with your yoga breath and simply listen to the breath, feel the breath and BE the breath. Sit for about five minutes. Be comfortable on the floor or on a chair or your yoga mat. Set a timer for five minutes. Complete the five minutes in silence. Don't answer the cell phone. Turn it off and put it away out of sight. Do you have an old school timer? Use that. If not, turn cell phone to air plane mode and set timer. At the end you repeat today's mantra: I ACCEPT THE PERSON I HAVE BEEN. I ACCEPT THE PERSON I AM RIGHT NOW. I ACCEPT THE PERSON I AM BECOMING.

Day 7

LOVE, LOVE, LOVE, LOVE, LOVE, LOVE! This is the answer to everything! Yes, everything! You are love. You are born from love. And you will die and leave this body in the name of love. Ok, so some days you will forget this. You will forget love because you are too caught up in all what the material world has to offer. You will be caught up in other people's opinions and your ego's opinions. You will be caught up in holding on to "I am right" and you will be fighting against other people's wrongs (or what you see as wrong). You will be so caught up in what is not important that you will forget what is important; LOVE! Your ego will win some days and it will give you a false sense of reality. We invite you back to LOVE by giving you this simple exercise. The moment you find yourself with a negative feeling in your body, find a mirror to stand in front of. You might want to find a mirror in a room where you can be by yourself. Or if you can't find that, go to the shared bath room and pretend you are putting on your make up, brushing your teeth or pretend you are checking yourself out in the mirror. Either way; find a mirror. When you stand in front of the mirror simply start repeating the following mantra out loud or in your mind: LOVE LOVE LOVE LOVE LOVE LOVE LOVE LOVE! Try repeating this mantra with a mad face! You won't be able to keep that up for very long. Because when you speak LOVE every cell in your body will feel LOVE! And love will be shown on your face with a big smile! Then say thank you to yourself and walk back into the material world.

Today's mantra: LOVE (repeat a thousand times)!

DAY 8

So what are the first few thoughts that enter your mind in the morning as you wake? How you hate your boss? How you hate how your boyfriend or girlfriend chews food? How you are so bitter towards your mom or dad for what they did in your childhood? So how will all those negative thoughts help you start your day off right? They won't. They will however help you set your day off wrong. Waking up on the wrong side of bed is a popular saying with you humans. You woke up with the wrong thoughts. So let's change the direction of your thoughts on this beautiful day. It is not about fixing your thoughts. It is about replacing negative thoughts with positive ones. So how do we do that? Easy! Wake up each morning with your gratitude list in your thoughts. Think of at least three things you are thankful and grateful for on this beautiful day. Perhaps it is being thankful for the sunshine outside or the calming sound of rain on your window. Maybe you are grateful for the pet sleeping by your feet or the wonderful children you will be waking up with. You might feel you are grateful for opportunities known and unknown this day. Perhaps you are longing for that great opportunity at work and you keep saying thank you each morning. Perhaps that promotion went to someone else. That doesn't mean that your time giving thanks is not working. It only means that something better is coming your way. You are not smarter than the Universe. It might be a better day or month or year for your promotion and it might be an even better opportunity waiting for you. So keep going at your gratitude list. Because you will always get what you need. So let's start being grateful right now. Start your list as you wake up and keep reminding yourself throughout your day to think of things to be grateful for. As we say thanks in our minds we attract more opportunities to be grateful for. So what if you can't think of anything to be grateful for (even though we know you can think of at least one thing)? We got you covered! Simply repeat today's mantra….which is: THANK YOU!

DAY 9

We welcome you to be yourself. Why do you constantly try to be something you are not? You act in one way with some people and different with others. You speak and act as if you were a thousand different people. Isn't that exhausting? We would be exhausted if we did that. Be yourself. Be you. Be one voice. Have the same voice and be the same kind person with the guy washing your car at the dealership and the CEO of the same car dealership. Be you. We can't say it enough. This world you live in make you believe you need to be something you are not. So you dress up in fancy shoes (some that actually hurt your back!) and buy expensive bags with some logo or initials on and you are suddenly someone else. Does that bag give you status? And all that you do is based on your status. How will the guys at work see me now? How will I look in front of my ex-in laws if I pass by them with my new love? How will I look in front of my parents in that Mercedes Benz? You all think about your status result whenever you make a decision. What if you make your decisions based on how the outcome will make YOU feel? Will you feel happy carrying that purse down Fifth Avenue? Will you be happy holding the hand of your new lover that you only picked because of his or her status? What if your decisions came from your heart? What if you asked the Universe to guide you to make decisions for the higher good and in the name of Love? What if that would be your agenda? Pretty nice agenda, we say.

Today's mantra: I FEEL GOOD ABOUT MYSELF TODAY!

DAY 10

Isn't it nice to be alive?! Right now say thank you for being alive! It is not something to take for granted. You only have today. Well, actually you only have right now. Cause in this moment nothing else exists. You haven't been to the future yet. You did your past. Stop dwelling there. Come up to speed and be here and now. So today and right now you are living. You are reading these words. You can't be anywhere else. You try so hard; in your mind all the time travelling from past to future and back again. Wow, we feel tired simply speaking of it. And you live like this daily! Take a deep breath, feel your breath and look up. What do you see? Doesn't matter if you see a beautiful blue sky or angry clouds or the ceiling in your office. What do you see? Simply observe the details above you. Now look down towards your feet. How are your feet? What are they touching? What do you feel under your feet? Perhaps take those shoes and socks off and let your feet feel themselves as they touch the ground. Or give your feet a massage. Simply observe your surroundings without judging them and without feeling irritation. Observe one thing and then the next. You are living in the now right now. Feels good, huh? As you observe your surroundings without judgment you can be where it is happening – right now. Do this exercise daily. Stop in your day and look up and look down and look around. What do you see?

Today's mantra: I AM PRESENT IN THE NOW.

DAY 11

Hello. It is a new day. So let's make the most of it. You might have had days where you were just lying in bed not wanting to come out from under the covers. You felt a hole in your belly or a feeling of unease in every cell. Most people have had this feeling once or twice or more. Some have this feeling for years. You can stop feeling this way by deciding the energy of your day. How do you decide the energy of your day? Simple. You start by taking charge of the energy within by controlling your words in your mind; what we call thoughts. Decide what energy you want to attract right now by saying some simple sentences in your mind. As you wake up start by saying this: THANK YOU FOR THIS BEAUTIFUL DAY! TODAY WILL BE A WONDERFUL DAY! I WAKE UP WITH LOVE AND I WALK WITH LOVE AND I LIVE WITH LOVE! THANK YOU! As we have said before; love is the strongest and highest there is. Nothing IS beyond love! Love IS! As you move throughout your day and feel that uneasy feeling in your gut sneak in, stop in your tracks, take a deep belly breath, look up and say in your mind (our out loud if it makes your heart sing): TODAY IS A BEAUTIFUL DAY! THIS IS TRUTH! THANK YOU! So what is today's mantra? You have already vibrated it!

DAY 12

Will you be honest with yourself? Will you tell yourself what your character defects are? Because all humans have them. Every single human have character defects. Some more than others. Some quite horrible. And some are not so big. All character defects can be let go of. If you want to. You simply have to be willing to let your character defects go. It is easier for you humans to point fingers at someone else. Often you get upset at others when they act in a way that is caused by the root of a character defect you also have. But instead of looking at yourself, you keep being upset at the other person. So let's take a look at you today. What is something with you that you wish you could let go of? Perhaps your ego gets hurt when someone gives you constructive criticisms. Perhaps that reminds you of not feeling good enough as a child? When you feel that uneasy feeling in your gut and your throat and your mind, and you start to feel resentment and anger.....then you have something to look at. Why do you get those feelings? Is someone pointing out the truth about you? And you don't want to admit the truth? You don't want to be honest with yourself? When you don't want to be honest with yourself you experience a burst of emotions and you start to defend yourself. And you should always know that when that feeling comes, it will be smart to stop and take a breath and count to ten before speaking. Because those words will always be there if you spit them out. You can't physically take those words back. So let's be honest. What pushes your ego buttons? Is it a look, a word, an action? Or is it a lack of a look, word or action that triggers you? We can't say it enough – take time every day in silence on your yoga mat or meditation pillow. If only for five minutes. In silence ask your Source what you can let go of. And let the answers flow. Listen to them without judging them and then let go.

Today's mantra: I LET GO!

DAY 13

Be with people that give you that happy feeling when you leave their company. Be with people that encourage you to live your dreams and to dream bigger. Be with people that are smarter than you! Yes, you heard it right. Be with people that are smarter than you. This is your goal even if you are a leader at something. This should be a very important goal *especially* if you are a leader. If you as a leader at something are the best and smartest person in the room, how are you supposed to grow? You want to keep growing. Which means you need to keep learning. You never stop learning. And one of your goals should be to always want to learn more. As a leader of what you lead surround yourself with people smarter than you and watch your world grow. One of the greatest things you can do for yourself is to open your arms and heart to the Universe and say: I KNOW NOTHING! It is in this state that you are most open to learning. And this is when the Universe will send you amazing opportunities to grow both personally and professionally. Don't walk around pretending to be a know-it-all. Because you can't know it all. If you did you would lead the world. Not just one country; you would lead the WORLD. And you would be the best there ever was at leading a planet. You are not leading a planet right now, and you won't this lifetime. However, you will be able to lead your community, your area and even your country if you so wish. There is growth when you admit to yourself you are not the smartest in the world. And you are not smarter than the Universe. You might act like that sometimes. And that is when you get yourself in trouble. Be open to learning every day and see your world grow!

Today's mantra (with open arms and an open heart): I AM WILLING TO LEARN!

DAY 14

Your life. Your answers. Why do you so often go to other people for guidance? "What do you think I should do?" you ask. "What should I say, do or not do?" It is very hard for someone else to tell you or even suggest what you should do as they see everything from their perspective in life. So you are stuck in a situation and you ask a friend for advice and that friend gives you an advice and you follow it. Now you are living through your friend's perspective. Because of your friend's traumatic child hood or troubled youth or failed marriages, that friend will of course only be able to give you advice based on how that friend sees the world. So if you would have sat down in meditation and silence and asked your own soul the questions, then you might have found other answers spoken – your truth. In fact we are pretty sure of it. You take two different people and put them into the same situation and there are two human beings with two totally different experiences and feelings about the very same situation. Therefore it is very difficult for you to be able to understand another human being's experience of life. We often hear you say "I understand how of you feel!". We say you cannot. And no one can understand how you feel as only you know how you feel. Because only you are on the inside of you. No one else. It is great to have a few core friends. And it is great to talk with them and listen to how they would do things in their shoes. And to listen to how they do things in their current life situation. You can draw major inspiration from talks like that. The difference here is that you are listening to them speaking about how they do things and handle things in their life. And perhaps you can borrow some of the same strategies and ways of doing things into your life. Perhaps they will work for you, perhaps they won't. But you should never make a decision based on what other people think you should do. And if you did make that decision based on another human beings perspective and acted on it based on other people's truths and had a bad gut feeling about it before you took action…..well, then all we can say is: YOU SHOULD HAVE LISTENED TO YOU!!!

Today's mantra: I TRUST MYSELF!

DAY 15

Remember when everything was pure and innocent? Perhaps you remember a time in your childhood or later in life when all was pure? What made your life not pure? Lies you tell yourself and others, we answer. All humans lie at some point in their lives. We understand you have a saying that certain lies are ok. Little white lies they are called. We want to share with you that a lie is a lie. The only one ok to tell is to save someone's life, including yours. So if you are dealing with a life or death situation it is ok to lie. The Universe will not punish your for that lie; you helped someone (the Universe never punishes. There is only attraction to energies. You humans like to think you will punished by a "bad" choice. We tell you the Universe is only love). And the energy of helping someone is a good one. Now, you tell lies all the time. You tell lies to return merchandise or get your money back. You tell lies to your spouse and children of your whereabouts. You tell lies to your bosses, coworkers, family and friends. Sometimes you hear yourself telling a lie almost like it wasn't even you saying it. Why do you lie? You lie to make yourself look good. And sometimes you have lied for so long it is just something that is a part of you. So you start to believe your lies. This is a very easy way to give you a disease. There is nothing about lying (unless saving a life) that gives ease and balance in your body. Your cells hear every word you speak and if those words are out of alignment of who you really are….well, then everything is off balance. And after years and years of lying and causing much drama in your life (because lies cause drama and it starts to get hard to keep up with all the stories), your body will start to talk to you to tell you that you are off balance. The body says you are far from ease. You are now at dis-ease level and the body wants you to create balance again. Just like your body felt and lived at one point in your life – when everything was pure and innocent. We wish for you to live from this place of being pure and innocent. So start today by making a choice to let go of those lies. Start speaking and acting your truth. You might have some cleaning up to do. It might be a really big job for you. So be patient with you. It will take cleaning up one room at a time before the whole house gets clean. Start today.

Today's mantra: I AM TRUTH!

DAY 16

So that irritating person is following you, right?! That
irritating person is at your work place, in your volunteer
group, at the grocery store, at the pool and on the same floor
in your apartment building. You see that irritating person
every day! How irritating, you say. You want to stop meeting
that irritating person, don't you?! We will teach you how.
As always and as everything is, it is simple. The irritation is
coming from you. Yes, that is right! You! There is nothing
wrong with that other person. And there is nothing wrong
with you. You simply need to remember your truth. When
you meet an irritating person or the person that gives you
that feeling, it is because that person has something you
don't like and you have it too! There is something inside
you that you wish to let go off. You simply haven't done
it yet. The Universe will send you many opportunities to
observe what it is you want to let go off by sending you
what you call an irritating person. That irritating person
is a blessing from the Universe. You meet these people as
long as you are holding on to whatever it is that you wish
to let go off. So next time you meet that irritating person,
simply observe and listen to your soul. Why don't you like
this person? What is it that person is doing or saying that
you don't like? Because whatever you don't like about them,
you don't like about yourself. You two are the same. Wow!
That hurt your ego to hear, didn't it? So do you want to
listen to your ego, or your Source and truth? When you
decide to let go of that irritated feeling in presence of an

irritating person …..those irritating people will no longer be in your presence. Perhaps they moved, or got a new job or simply stopped being irritating. Not because they changed, but because you changed something inside of you. You decided to not let that irritating thing or person bother you anymore. Perhaps you simply look the other way or perhaps you simply started to say thank you to the Universe for the opportunities to let go of something it was time to let go of. The Universe wouldn't show you these opportunities if you weren't ready for change. It is hard for you human beings, we know, to let go of irritation. It is easier to say it is the other person's fault that you are feeling irritated. We wish you would try this practice. When that irritating person arrives into your reality, in your mind say thank you for the lesson. Today's mantra….there is none. We simply want you to observe yourself today and to observe your feelings. That's today's lesson. Be your own truth.

DAY 17

So you want to meet some nice people? You want to meet some happy people? Some patient people? Are you tired of meeting impatient, moody and angry people every day? If you answered yes to one or two or all questions, we invite you to look at yourself. What kind of person are YOU? Happy, smiley, patient, kind, generous, honest? The qualities you have and hold are the kind of people you will attract yourself. So you can blame yourself for the people you meet daily. If you meet someone grumpy, mean and dishonest, you can blame yourself for meeting that person. If you meet someone happy, kind and generous, you can blame yourself for meeting that person. When you meet people you like, say 'thank you' in your mind. Say thank you so you will meet more people like that. When you meet people you don't like, in your mind say 'I let you go'. There is something of you in everyone you meet. So be careful with what energy you wake up with. Because that will decide the kind of interactions you will have that day. Watch your thoughts as they help guide your day. A wonderful mantra you can repeat in your mind as you wake and before you go to work, or school or into that meeting you have been dreading is this : TODAY I ONLY MEET WONDERFUL, KIND, HAPPY AND HONEST PEOPLE!

DAY 18

So the time is NOW to do something about your dream. The big mistake is to think there is so much time. Time is an illusion anyway. You need to know that NOW is just as good as any time to act on that calling from your heart. You know those words that you keep hearing in your mind and they feel so good in your heart? Those are whispers from your soul. Your soul is telling you what it longs to do. As a human being you are not taught to listen to those whispers. No one ever told you about those messages from within. You didn't have those teachers growing up. You have them NOW. Those messages from within will not stop coming until you take action. You see, there is only one time to take action.....that time is NOW. You might think we mean that you should have that big fancy house, that shiny new car, a great family, a great social life and amazing career all at once. No, that is not what we mean. And for most humans that is an illusion. You can have it all, yes. But not all at once. So as you are enjoying the new life with a new born, you won't be feeling the call to be going out knocking on doors at those companies that you dream to work for. Feeling motivated to start a new career most likely won't come between changing diapers and trying to get some sleep in. As you are enjoying being in love with that wonderful new person in your life you might not feel the call for working sixty hours a week. Then you are feeling for filling your free time with walks in the park, dinner dates, long weekend getaways and just hanging out doing nothing. Those callings from within for the big changes will come at the right time (and becoming a parent and falling in love were also callings for change from your heart). And when that time comes it will be called NOW. And when those messages from within keep repeating, then NOW is the time to take action towards those dreams. You will hear the whispers when it is the right time. If it wasn't the right time you wouldn't hear the whispers.

Today's mantra: I LIVE IN THE NOW!

DAY 19

Please know that you have the power to create something from one small thought. Every thought you have will become. Thoughts are like wishes. What you think you wish for. Whether you want that to become or not, each thought will become. So now that you know this truth; what will you think about today? No one among you humans speak of this. Except in the elite class. We are now making this information accessible to all. Your thoughts will create your future. What you are living right now is caused by your thinking in the past. We want you to know that it all starts with a thought. Your thought becomes a word, your word becomes an action, that action becomes a habit, and all your habits become your character, and your character defines your life. So start your day in meditation with a strong focus on controlling what is in your mind. Perhaps it is your gratitude list, perhaps it is your visualization about your future or simply say thank you over and over again. We know you humans get caught up in negative thinking that causes fear. We know this creates problems for you in your life. We wish for you to release this kind of thinking. We want for you to start using your thoughts as your wishes. Because they are wishes. So should you walk around thinking mad thoughts about everything your spouse or partner does wrong or what they don't do? Why would anything except what you think/wish come true? Why would you wish for someone to not treat you right? Of course you wouldn't seem to be the right answer......yet at the same time you do as you see/think negative situations in your mind! So stop thinking about people not treating you right. Start thinking/wishing for someone to treat you right. Perhaps that person should be you? Think/wish you being nice to you. Think/wish you living your dreams (no one is telling you that you can't live your dreams except you. Other people's words are only their truth.). Think/wish happy thoughts. Wish yourself the best wishes! Just like you wish good for others (We know you sometimes wish bad for others. We can hear your thoughts.). And you receive back what you think/wish. Start wishing for a life with purpose, joy, happiness and LOVE!

Today's mantra: I WISH HAPPINESS FOR MYSELF!

DAY 20

Let this be a reminder to you that you are in charge of your feelings towards others. You and only you decide how you feel about all the people you interact with daily. So there is this one person, right, that always gets you to feel unease in the belly whenever that person comes in the same room as you. You do whatever you can to circle the room so that you won't interact with that person that makes you feel so nervous. However, as you think/wish that you won't interact with that person…..you will get just what you think of the most…..THAT person. And it will seem like that person always ends up talking to you. This kind of person exists for most people. So should you try to avoid this person the rest of your life? No! You need to change how you feel about this person. You cannot change that person. Not even one bit. So let go of that impossible mission right now! However; you can change your world by what you think of when you interact with this person. Next time you meet that person that you so wish to avoid (do you see that this person will be in your life as long as you think of this person?) practice the following practice. When faced with a person that makes you feel uneasy, think of him or her as a little child. That child was very likely hurt by some adults or peers. Perhaps that person was abused by caregivers. If that is the case, that person holds lots of anger, sadness, resentment and hate locked up inside. This person might take those feelings out on you at work or any other setting you meet this person. So think of this hurt little boy or girl when this person speaks to you. Be silent. Be quiet. Listen to that person talk and talk and talk. All the while inside your mind you are sending love to this little hurt child. And you wish this little child all the love a child deserves and needs. You smile to that child from your heart and you smile with your face to the adult standing in front of you. Practice this and you will be amazed at the change of feeling YOU will have about this person. Or perhaps this person simply won't be in your life anymore as your energy has changed. Their hurt energy does not match with your loving energy. So you won't meet often or even any more. That person hasn't changed anything about him or herself. You have changed you.

Breathe in and send love to you. Breathe out and send love to someone who needs it….in this case the person in front of you. And that is your work for this day.

DAY 21

Why aren't you speaking to us? Why aren't you asking? We are waiting for your questions! As you rise in the morning go into your meditation and ask us to guide you this beautiful day. No, you don't have to have a fancy meditation room or even a Zen looking meditation pillow. You can ask us from your bed. You can ask us as you are brushing your teeth (make brushing your teeth your meditation). We are waiting for you to ask. When you ask we will answer. When you ask we will go into action for you. However, if we don't hear from you we can't help you. And we are so ready to help. We are just sitting here doing nothing waiting for you. So ask us. Most of you don't even know what to ask for as your dreams have been silenced by the society you live in. The society that says that you can't mount to anything unless you come from the right family, the right neighborhood, the right school and so on. There is no right or wrong here, folks. Everything simply IS. So ask us to assist you in what you dream and hope and wish for. First step; get in touch with what you want. Dream some. Start small if dreaming big scares you. But please know that you can dream big as you don't need anyone's approval of that dream. Only you need to believe in it. But some of you will even doubt your own dream. We ask you to crush that doubt and start believing. Why would you doubt yourself? Then others will also doubt you. Believe in yourself! Believe in those whispers from your soul; those words you hear repeatedly. So sit down, lie down or stand up and ask us to show you how you can be of service for the greater good. Don't ask us for that shiny car or brand new bike. Ask us how you can help and serve the people you share this planet with. Ask us how you can help and serve the animals; the one's without a voice. Ask us how to be of good and we will show you the way. And perhaps the way will include that shiny car, a brand new home or a fast bike. Or perhaps something better. Simply ask us what you want us to assist you with and then open yourself up to receive.

Today's mantra is an asking: PLEASE SHOW ME WHAT I NEED TO DO THIS DAY TO SERVE THE GREATER GOOD! THANK YOU!

DAY 22

Be smart! What does that mean!? That means to listen to your higher calling; that inner voice. Do not listen to everyone else's opinion. We have touched on this before. However, this is a very important message and we cannot repeat it enough. Your inner guide, your soul, your truth will whisper you messages throughout your day. These are your reminders on what to do next. They are reminders on what action to take as your next step towards your happy life. Too often, and sometimes all the time, you go to others for approval for the action you wish to take. If you then hear doubt in other people's opinions about your truth, you too start to doubt your next step. And sometimes, and often all the time, you stop the process. You stop the next step. You stop your goal. You stop your dream! This is something that causes deep sorrow, regret and depression in many peoples' lives. Regret is poison. You will regret more what you didn't do then what you did and failed at. And truly, there are no failures. Every time you fall, or what you humans call failure, you are one step closer to success. Because from that fall you now know how NOT to do it next time. So next time that whisper from your soul/Source/inner wisdom speaks to you; don't go asking other people what they think of it. Just do it! Simply take action! Don't procrastinate. Jump into it. Go for it! Can we say it more? Can we say it in any other way? Probably, but we don't want to. We hope you get the message by now. You don't need anyone else's approval of your dream. This is your dream. This is your life. You have one shot at it. Jump. Run. Climb. Swim. Do what feels good to you. No one else knows what feels good to you. Only you know. So you need to start trusting those inner whispers. They are speaking from the Source. They are speaking from your truth. Your truth; not your spouse's truth, not your friend's truth, not your boss' truth. Your truth. Now go take some action.

Today's mantra: I TRUST MY INNER CALLING!

DAY 23

Let's take a journey. Let's take a journey through your life. We recommend and request that you do this lying down on your yoga mat, bed or couch. This will require your entire attention. As you lie down, find comfort and only comfort. If something feels painful or uncomfortable simply move your body until pain and discomfort disappear. Remember nothing lasts forever. So perhaps put a pillow under your head or a rolled up blanket under your knees or legs. Be comfortable. Even place a blanket over your belly and an eye pillow over your forehead and eyes (a simple wash cloth sprayed with some water and essential oils will do). Now close your eyes and let your body be at rest. Take some deep belly breaths. Start to simply observe your breath and let go of any reason why you think you should change your breath. Let your eye lids be heavy yet soft. Now allow yourself to start seeing in your mind when it all started; see your birth. How does your birth make you feel? Now move on into your newborn time. How does this make you feel? Stay in the feeling and the images that you see. Now move on to your toddler years, starting school, starting high school, starting college, starting adulthood and move all the way up to the current time. At each phase of your life, pause and let visions, feelings, imagery and thought all come to you. Push nothing away. Notice where things feel good and notice where things feel bad. Simply notice. As you have stayed with the present time about ten breaths in your meditation, start to walk toward your future. Create it in your mind with love, light, support, opportunities, peace, wealth, abundance and more love. Stay in that feeling. Take five to ten deep yoga breaths in that feeling and then blink your eyes about five times. Then slowly open your eyes. Let your body stay lying down for another ten deep belly breaths before you slowly rise up and put your feet on the ground with gratitude. You have just gone through your timeline and learnt about the times in your life when things were good and when things were challenging. And you discovered you are still here! Those challenging times didn't defeat you. They made you stronger! You rose up and you are empowered! You went to your future with the strongest creation; your own power and your own vision! Nothing can stop you from creating what you want! Nothing......! Now go on with your day. Enough for now.

DAY 24

So you have been hurt. Who hasn't? Have you ever met someone who never has been hurt or never had their ego defeated? If you have, then please demand them to write a book about living a life without being hurt. We don't think you will meet such a human being. So let's deal with this hurt person inside of you. At one time you were a small child; a little girl or a little boy. Someone hurt you by words or action. We have taught you to forgive yourself and forgive others. Let's now LOVE that small child, youth or young adult that got hurt. It doesn't matter at what level you got hurt. Your hurt is real to you. Just because someone else got hurt in a much worse way than you it doesn't mean that you are not entitled to your feelings. You are entitled your feelings and emotions. They are real to you. So let's begin. In your meditation today visualize that little child you once were. If your hurt happened as a child, stay there. If your hurt happened at an older age, go there. See the young you that got hurt. Now YOU, as the present you, go to that young you and hold around the young version of you. You simply hold the past version of you and say: "Everything will be okay. Everything will be great. You are a fighter. You are strong. You are loved. You are protected. You are good enough." You might want to repeat these words a few times to the past you in order for the message to get through. When you feel your message has been received, simply say this: "Farewell for now. We will meet again and everything will be wonderful then. You got this and I am here for you."

Then visualize you leaving the young version of yourself. Come back to your body, smile to yourself and say a thank you to yourself. Now open your eyes. You can always do this meditation whenever you feel you haven't healed some past wounds. We even want to say that you cannot do this meditation enough. It will heal you in a magical way. It will heal you in a way words cannot describe. Enjoy the healing.

Today's mantra: I AM HEALED!

DAY 25

Exercise your right to be silent. Set up a weekly silent day. Or perhaps once a month if weekly is too challenging for your life. What is a silent day? It is a day of no speaking. People can speak to you. However you do not speak back. A simple way to make this doable is to take a small piece of paper and write the words "I AM IN SILENCE". Then take the piece of paper and pin it to your shirt or jacket. This way you can refer to the note when you are home with the family or out at the grocery store. A great day for silent day is Sunday. You might be done with the week's shopping. Your family might have a day trip to the park planned. Perhaps you choose to go to the ball game alone. It is ok to be in silence when the rest of the world is chatting away. You are not missing out on anything being silent. Actually you might find that you are gaining more than you thought you would. You will gain the peace within that comes from being in silence. You will hear MORE; the sounds around you will be clearer and you will notice sounds you normally take for granted. Or perhaps you even have forgotten the sounds were there. You will acknowledge the fact that the sounds have their right to be there. You will lose the need to be irritated over sounds and noise. You will appreciate the silence inside the whirl wind of sounds around you. Enjoy not speaking for 24 hours. Enjoy seeing the world through different eyes….and in this case; through different ears. You will find that your world is exciting and new and perhaps you will discover new gratitude for your life. We wish you good luck. Enjoy! Make it a weekly or monthly practice. If in your life a whole 24 hours of silence is impossible (perhaps you are a parent of a baby or small children…then we understand 24 hours of no talking is challenging), take two to four hours out of your Sunday or one day a month of silence. Take a walk around town with your sign of silence and answer no one. Step onto an unknown path in the woods and discover new worlds with both your eyes and ears. There is so much for you to enjoy on this planet. Listen to your planet. Be well. Be silent.

Today's mantra: THANK YOU FOR SILENCE!

DAY 26

It is your inner truth to be truthful. The world as you know it (and as we know it through your eyes) is so filled with untruths. We do not understand this. As the Indian man was confused by the lies of the white man, so are we confused by the lies told by the humans. Why would you say one thing, and then go ahead and do the opposite? How does that not affect your health? The body must be confused. The mind is constantly living lies. The body is constantly on paths going away from the truth of the soul. The body wants to be united with mind and soul. It is there the body is in it's natural balance. When the body is dragged opposite direction of soul by untruthful thoughts.....well, then there are just too many things out of balance....and there must one day be dis-ease. Perhaps that dis-ease and imbalance come as feeling tired all the time, chronic exhaustion, muscle pain, headache, and dizziness and so on. If you, dear human, do not take these signs of imbalances seriously and you keep going at the same pace....well, one day you will hit the wall or sometimes the ground literally.....and you will find yourself in the hospital. We encourage you to carefully listen to your body. It speaks to you with a great and intelligent voice every second of the day. Do not ignore these messages. Too many humans have in the past and they are no longer here. They went too soon. Listen to your body. The aches and pains are messages to you. Something is out of balance. One of the most powerful ways you can find back to your balance is to start speaking truth. Truth to yourself and others. Speak the truth even though you might think you'll lose something. If telling a lie makes you think you will be able to hold on to something or someone....then you are already living a lie inside your mind. And that lie/illusion is making you sick. Listen to your heart, your mind, your soul, your body. Everything is connected......from your thoughts and your words to your blood, muscles, bones and organs. Every cell in your body listens to your thoughts and your words. Speak the truth and enjoy good health! This is such an important message. Therefore we visit this subject as often as we can so you will get the message. Please listen. We are here to assist you in enjoying good health. That is your body's natural place.

Today's mantra: I AM TRUTH SO THEREFORE I AM HEALTHY!

DAY 27

Be nice to yourself! What does that mean? Oh, how we could write book after book on that subject. This world needs the following message; YOU DESERVE ALL YOUR DREAMS COME TRUE AND MORE! Inside most of you human beings we find a belief that is pushing you down. This belief says that you are not good enough. You are not alone feeling this way. Millions of you feel this way deep down inside. It is a toxic belief. As long as you hold this toxic belief it will be very hard, if not impossible, for you to be nice to you. When you hold this belief of not deserving the best in life you will continue attracting people, situations and circumstances that will CONFIRM that you are not deserving of good. It might be that you attract that horrible spouse or lover time and time again. It might be that you attract that bullying boss or co-worker. It might be that you attract dead end jobs. It might be that you attract that mean land lord. So how do you change this type of attraction? We have spoken often about this tool in which you can change what you attract; your thinking! It is inside your own mind that you will set the pace of this change. It is inside you own mind that you can change your world. Start telling yourself that you deserve all your dreams come true and more. Start telling yourself that you deserve that loving and respectful spouse or lover or friend. Start telling yourself that you are deserving of LOVE in every area of your life. Start telling yourself nice things. Become your own mentor. We wish for you so deeply that you realize as soon as possible that you are WORTHY and DESERVING of LOVE, WEALTH, HAPPINESS, GOOD HEALTH, ABUNDANCE, PEACE, SAFETY, JOY, LAUGHTER and ALL GOOD FEELING EMOTIONS! Here is a powerful mantra we encourage you to repeat throughout your day:

I DESERVE LOVE IN EVERY AREA OF MY LIFE! I AM WORTHY! I AM GOOD ENOUGH!

DAY 28

What are you feeling right now? Allow yourself to FEEL. So many people will tell you to control your feelings; stop being so angry; don't be so sad all the time; don't be such a push-over; get over it; grow some tough skin! You often hear that you should bottle up your emotions and not even show them. This is something you might have been taught from early on in childhood. We are here to tell you that you don't have to control your feelings or even bottle them up inside. You need to control your thoughts! You see; your feelings are your guidance system. Your feelings show you what you are thinking. A negative feeling in your body indicates a negative thought. A positive feeling in the body indicates a positive thought. Feelings come from thoughts. We have often shared with you of the importance about thought. It all starts with thought. EVERYTHING starts with thought. And we are not interested in hearing any of your excuses about how difficult it is for you to control your thoughts. You see; it is easy to be inside your comfort zone, but absolutely nothing grows there. NOTHING! If you want change, you have to change everything. And the most important thing you have to change is your thinking. How do I do this, you ask? We answer; on your meditation pillow, on your yoga mat, on your walk in the forest or by the water, as you drive your car, as you stand in line the grocery store, as you cook your food......as you live your life. Anytime you have time to be with your thoughts; take control of what words are allowed to travel around in your mind and from your mind to your body. This is so important! This information can change your life! *IF* you choose to take action. Just as you choose to put your feet on the ground in the morning and walk to the bathroom to freshen up – choosing your thoughts is also an action. It doesn't become less of an action just because it is not on the outside. In fact; the most important action you will ever take is the one on the inside. So let's get started!

Today's mantra: I AM IN CONTROL OF MY THOUGHTS!

DAY 29

Your words tell you what you are thinking. Simply listen, really listen, to what comes out of your mouth as you speak to others. Then you hear your own truth. Or perhaps you hear lack of truth. Either way you are speaking your thoughts. It is often difficult to stop in the middle of a sentence when you catch yourself telling a lie. But we encourage you to stop if you catch yourself speaking something that is different and separate from your Source. It is ok to say: "Sorry, I just lied. Let me correct that." You won't lose your face. You will gain your respect. So often you are used to speaking what you think is your truth as you believe your negative thoughts. But as you start to meditate, practice yoga, take care of yourself….it will be more and more difficult to think and speak negative words. Speaking words that are loving and caring will be more and more the norm. Because the more you work with yourself, the more you will release the ego and negative thoughts. And you will create a bigger and bigger ball of positive thoughts and therefore your words will also be more positive. Don't be discouraged. It takes time to break habits. So don't demand perfectionism for yourself. Demand progression. Notice your words, and when some words fly out of your mouth that you don't like….you can pause and start over again. You can always start over again. So listen carefully to yourself as you go about your day interacting with people. Are you speaking your dreams and goals? Or are you speaking your lack, your doubts, and your fears? We encourage you so much to meditate and practice yoga as these are great tools to move away from negative thinking, speaking and acting. These tools are given to you on this planet in almost every country. Take advantage of this practice if you feel your thinking is a bit on the negative side. You all will have negative thoughts, and therefore negative words, from time to time. The goal for you should be to create the ball of positivity to be much bigger than the ball of negativity. Your progress will be reflected in your words.

Today's mantra: I SPEAK FROM MY SOURCE!

DAY 30

The future is yours to create. Everything you see in front of you right now you have created. It is created through and by thought. How do you create your dream world in the future? First, be grateful for what you have right now. And then write down what you want to continue to be grateful for in the future. Perhaps there are new things, people, circumstances and experiences you would like to be thankful for in the future. Write them down as well. The writing process is a powerful process. Every day we suggest you journal in your gratitude journal. It can be a beautiful journal you purchase at the book store or a simple note book. Use a blue inked pen. This is effective as the color blue has many spiritual symbolic meanings. Simply Google this. Yes, we know about Google. So write down your gratitude list each morning, or each evening, or both. No limits, please. Be bold and dream big. Dream so super big and be proud of your dreams. It is our experience as we have observed humans that this process of journaling is highly effective. We witness dreams come true daily this way. Journaling is a practice. It is something you need to train yourself to do. It is not something that will come easy or natural at first unless you have done it for years. Do not expect yourself to do perfect right away. And it is never about perfectionism in anything in life. It is about progress. And progress you will find through practice. Practice is doing something over and over again until it becomes natural to your being. Get that journal and pen ready right now and write down your dreams and wishes with a big THANK YOU in front of it. So you write it as if it already IS. You see, the Universe doesn't know the difference if it is a dream/wish or happening right now. The Universe sees all as if it already IS. And when you are clear of doubt and fear.....and when you believe and have faith in the process....and when you are open to becoming the best version of you....and when you accept all that you are......and when you believe with all your cells that you are good enough for your dreams...then, and only then, will your dreams as written in your journal come true. Have fun with it! Play with it! Enjoy it! It's just life.......

Todays' mantra: I DESERVE MY DREAMS!

MY DREAM MAP

This is my very own place for creation. I can write down
my dreams and goals, inspirational quotes or messages
from my Source. I can also cut out clippings from
magazines and catalogues and glue or tape them to the
following pages. On these pages I will create my future.

Printed in the United States
By Bookmasters

Printed in the United States
By Bookmasters